HOW TO BE A BIG BROTHER

HOW TO BE A BIG BROTHER

A GUIDE TO BEING THE BEST OLDER SIBLING EVER

BY ASHLEY MOULTON

Illustrations by Kavel Rafferty

ROCKRIDGE PRESS

For general information on our other products and services or to obtain technical support, please contact our Customer Care Department within the United States at (866) 744-2665, or outside the United States at (510) 253-0500.

Rockridge Press publishes its books in a variety of electronic and print formats. Some content that appears in print may not be available in electronic books, and vice versa.

Interior and Cover Designers: Matt Girard and Tricia Jang
Art Producer: Meg Baggot
Editor: Erum Khan
Production Manager: Jose Olivera
Production Editor: Melissa Edeburn

Illustrations © Kavel Rafferty, 2020

ISBN: Print 978-1-64739-140-9
eBook 978-1-64739-141-6

R0

To Justin:
Thanks for making me an
expert big "stister."

Welcome to Big Brotherhood!

Dear Big Brother,

Congratulations! You are about to level up. Soon, you'll have a very special superpower . . . Big Brother Power!

You might have a lot of questions about what that means, like: *Will I still get to do fun things with my parent? Will the baby steal all my toys? When can we play hide-and-go-seek?* Don't worry! This book is filled with tips from us, your fellow big brothers. We are boys just like you who have gone through this big change.

Having a new baby sibling is fun. Because you're a big kid, you'll be able to help take care of them. Before you know it, you will have a special friend to play with any time you want.

Big brothering is awesome, but it also means that things are changing. That is totally normal. Your family will be different than it was before, and sometimes that can be hard. It's all part of growing up.

We can be *your* big brothers and share what it was like when we became big brothers. All our families are different, but we all have one thing in common: We started off being just regular boys, and then we got Big Brother superpowers.

By the time you're finished reading this book, you'll be ready to be the best big brother ever!

CHAPTER 1

BEFORE BABY ARRIVES

The time before a new baby arrives is so exciting! Your family will be busy getting ready, and everyone will be looking forward to meeting the newest family member. There are many ways you can start being a great big brother even before the baby comes.

Jamal Goes to the Doctor

Jamal got to see his baby sibling for the first time today . . . well, sort of! Jamal's sibling was growing inside his mom's tummy. The only way to "see" the baby was through a special doctor's test called an ultrasound.

Jamal went to the doctor's appointment with his mom. When they got there, the doctor squeezed a clear goo on his mom's stomach. The doctor touched the ultrasound wand to Jamal's mom's tummy. This wand was kind of like magic. It showed a picture of the baby on a screen, even though the baby was still inside Jamal's mom! The doctor moved the ultrasound wand around to see the baby from different angles and to make sure the baby was healthy.

The picture was pretty fuzzy, so Jamal was not really sure what he was seeing until the doctor pointed to the outline of the baby's body. Jamal put his hand on mom's tummy, and he could even feel the baby kick! Jamal still had no idea what his sibling looked like, but he knew one thing: There was definitely a baby in there! He was so excited that he would meet the baby soon.

Noah Meets Someone New

It was a big day for Noah's family. It was their adoption home visit day! A social worker was coming to their house to meet Noah's family. A social worker is someone who helps families who want to adopt a child.

First, the social worker took a tour of the house. They needed to make sure that everything would be safe for a new baby. Then, it was time for the social worker to ask Noah questions. It made Noah nervous. The social worker explained that Noah couldn't give any wrong answers, so that made him feel better. Most of the questions were easy to answer, like "How do you feel about having a new brother or sister?" (Excited!) and "What are your parents like?" (They love me very much!)

A few months passed while the adoption agency was finding a baby for Noah's family. One day, his parents got an exciting phone call. They had been matched with a baby girl and would get to bring her home in a few weeks. Noah was so excited he couldn't stand it! He looked at his new sister's picture every day while he waited to meet her.

What Can We Do Together?

Your family will be very busy getting ready for the new baby, and there's a lot you can do to help! Here are some ideas:

Make something special for the baby. Make something for the baby's space, like a painting, a toy, or a blanket.

Help set up the baby's space. Pick out art to hang on the wall, help your parent build the crib, and unpack gifts.

Get the baby's clothes ready. Pick out a special outfit the baby can wear during their first day home. Help sort hand-me-down clothes into different sizes. Hang tiny outfits in the closet. Decide which outfit you would like to wear if it came in your size!

Help pick the baby's name. With your parent, look through a baby name book or website, and write down your favorite names. Just for fun, also write down the silliest names you find.

Sing to the baby. Did you know that babies can hear things even before they are born? If you sing a special song over and over to your sibling, they might even recognize it once they are born!

What Do I Think?

Now that you've read this chapter, it's a great time to think about any questions you might have about becoming a big brother. We've written some questions to get you started, but you can add more. You can think about your answers, write them down, or talk about them with your family.

What am I most looking forward to when I become a big brother?

What makes me most nervous about becoming a big brother?

What will the baby be like? How will they act?

What things will our family need to do to get ready for the baby? How can I help?

CHAPTER 2

BECOMING A BIG BROTHER

You're ready to become a big brother, and now the special day is here! There are many ways for a baby to join a family. No matter how it happens in your family, it will be a day you'll never forget.

Omar Visits His Nana

Omar's parents woke him up and said, "Today you're going to meet your sister!" Omar's mom was going to the hospital to have her baby. Before his parents went to the hospital, they dropped Omar off at his grandmother's house.

Omar and his nana had fun baking cookies while they were waiting for his sister to be born. Finally, after what seemed like forever, they got an exciting phone call. Omar was officially a big brother!

Nana and Omar drove to the hospital, and a nurse told them which room to go to. Omar's mom was resting in a bed, and his teeny tiny sister was in a special baby bed next to her. To help Omar hold his sister, Nana put a pillow in Omar's lap and carefully placed his sister in Omar's arms. Omar couldn't believe she was finally here!

Mateo Stays Home

Mateo's mom was ready to have her baby, so she called the midwife and said it was time. A midwife is someone who helps people give birth.

The midwife came to their house and Mateo helped her bring her things inside. Mateo's mom was doing a lot of hard work because her body was getting ready to have the baby. To help her, Mateo brought her water to drink and rubbed her back.

After a while, the midwife said that it was time for the baby to come and asked Mateo to wait in his room. Mateo played by himself for a while. Then he heard a baby crying. The midwife brought Mateo back in the room, and he saw the baby lying on his mom's chest. He was so small and cute! Mateo walked over and gave him a big-brother kiss.

Daniel Meets His New Sibling

Daniel's parents wanted to be foster parents. This meant that they wanted to be a temporary family for kids whose parents couldn't take care of them. When Daniel's family signed up, they weren't sure when a foster child would come to live with them or how old the child would be. One day they got a phone call that a toddler would be coming to live with them in a few hours. They had to make a quick trip to the store to get clothes and supplies.

Daniel was waiting nervously when he heard a knock at the door. When he and his parents answered it, they found a social worker holding the hand of his new foster sister. Daniel waved hello and helped give her a tour of their house. He read his foster sister a book he had made for her all about their family. He hoped his new foster sister would like it here!

What Can We Do Together?

It can be hard waiting for a baby to arrive. Here are some things you can do to pass the time while you're waiting to meet your new sibling:

Make a welcome poster. Do you know the baby's name yet? Make a giant poster that says "Welcome home, (name)!" and hang it on the door to your house.

Make a book about your family. Help your sibling get to know your family by making a picture book about the people in your family, where you live, and things you like to do together. Draw your pictures on plain paper, punch holes on one side, and put the pages in a binder or tie it together with string.

Pick out a stuffed animal for the baby. Ask the grown-up that is waiting with you to help you pick out a new stuffed animal. You can also wash one of your stuffed animals to give to the baby.

Bake cookies. With a grown-up, make a batch of cookies for your parent. Your parent might be really tired, and delicious cookies will help cheer them up!

Make a flower bouquet. Flowers are a nice way to tell your parent "Congratulations!" Make a bouquet of paper flowers or flowers you picked from a garden (after asking permission).

What Do I Think?

You might have some questions about what will happen when your sibling joins your family. Here are some questions you might want to ask your family. You can write down your own, too.

What will happen the day I get a sibling?

How long will it take for me to meet the baby?

Who will be taking care of me while I'm waiting?

Where will I be while I'm waiting?

CHAPTER 3

YOU'RE A BIG BROTHER!

Congratulations! You're a big brother now!
Here's how you can be a super big brother
for your brand-new sibling.

Nap Time

Babies sleep a lot! When they are first born, it will seem like your sibling is *always* sleeping. They even sleep during the day when you are wide awake.

After a few months, your sibling will stay awake for longer stretches during the day, but they will still need to take naps for a couple of years. This might be really annoying sometimes. Your family might have to stop what you're doing so your sibling can go home and take a nap. Try to remember that you are being an awesome big brother by helping your sibling get the sleep they need. Your sibling will also be less fussy when they get enough rest. You can use the quiet time to read, color, or play.

Super Safe Brother Tip

Always ask a grown-up before giving your sibling a blanket or a stuffed animal, especially when they are sleeping.

Feeding Baby

You might be excited to share some of your favorite foods with your sibling . . . but wait! They are only going to drink milk or formula for the first few months. They will start eating "solid food" eventually, but this food won't be very solid at all. Babies' first foods are soft because they are learning how to chew and swallow. Your sibling's first food might be something like mashed-up bananas or vegetables that have been blended smooth.

As they get older, they will learn how to eat different kinds of food. Soon you'll be able to eat the same yummy foods together!

Super Safe Brother Tip

Always ask a grown-up before giving a baby food or anything else they might put in their mouth.

Super Helper Brother Tip

It's hard for your parent to get up when they're feeding a small baby. You can take them things they need like a drink of water (for your parent) or a clean burp cloth (for the baby). Your parent might also teach you how to feed your sibling. When your sibling starts eating food, you can help them learn to like new foods by smiling and saying "yummy" when they try something new.

Changing Baby's Diapers

All the milk the baby drinks has to go somewhere! Your sibling won't know how to use the potty for a long time. They will use diapers instead. Babies need to have their diapers changed often, sometimes 12 times a day!

Super Helper Brother Tip

You can help your parent by handing them a clean diaper or a wipe, or by throwing away the dirty diaper. Sing a song to your sibling to help keep them calm while being changed.

Bath Time

Your baby sibling is so tiny they might take their first baths in the sink. Since babies can't sit up on their own, your sibling might use a special baby bathtub to help them stay safe. You can be a bath-time buddy by playing a gentle game of "splish-splash" when they are in the tub, or by gently pouring water on their arms and legs. Just be careful to watch out for their face! When your sibling gets older and stronger, they will be able to take bubble baths in the tub just like you.

Super Safe Brother Tip
There should always be a grown-up around when your sibling is in the bath.

Adventure Time

When it's time to do fun stuff with your family, your sibling needs help to get around. If you all have to drive somewhere, they will get strapped into a car seat in the backseat. Some babies don't like this very much. If your sibling doesn't like their car seat, try singing songs or making funny faces to distract them.

When you're walking somewhere, your sibling will need help since they can't walk yet. Often, they will get pushed in a stroller. Your parent might also carry them in a special baby backpack.

25

Playtime

You *will* be able to play with your sibling when they're a little baby, but you won't be climbing on the monkey bars with them in the beginning. It can be surprising when a baby is born because they don't know how to do much besides eat and sleep.

There is a lot your sibling has to learn before they can play. First, they will learn how to follow something with their eyes. Then they will learn how to move their arms and legs on purpose. Finally, they will learn how to hold a toy in their hand. Soon, your sibling will be rolling, crawling, and walking. Great news, big brother. You can help them learn how to do all these things! Playing with your sibling might be very different from how *you* play, but it is still really fun.

Super Safe Brother Tip

Be very gentle when playing with your sibling. Always ask a grown-up before holding them or picking them up.

Babies LOVE putting everything in their mouths, and you can help them play safely. Small toys are not safe for babies, so ask a grown-up before giving them anything to play with. Once your sibling is able to move around on their own, make sure you keep your small toys (like blocks, marbles, or doll accessories) away from them.

Wei Plays Gently

At first, Wei was disappointed when his newborn sister came home because she seemed pretty boring. But then he realized that he *could* play with his sister. He just had to play like a baby! Wei made funny faces and noises at her every day. When she was two months old, she started to smile back at him. A few weeks later, he made her laugh for the first time. Because he was so silly, he could make her laugh even when his parents couldn't. Wei felt proud of his special big brother silly power.

He wanted to teach his sister how to move her arms, so he asked his dad if he could hold things like rattles and stuffed animals near his sister's hands. One day, when she was three months old, he handed her a toy. To Wei's amazement, she could hold it! It was fun watching her learn.

Rohan Helps Baby Learn

Rohan's dad told him how his baby brother needed to do lots of "tummy time" so that his neck would get stronger. His dad placed his brother on his tummy on the floor. Rohan got down next to him and shook a rattle. "Come on, baby, look up here!" he said to encourage his brother.

As Rohan's brother got stronger, Rohan's new goal was to teach him to roll over. He held a toy just out of his brother's reach, and his brother kicked his legs to try to turn over. It was cute to watch him try a new skill!

Jordan Plays with Toys

Jordan loved playing with his brother now that he could sit up by himself and hold toys. Jordan's favorite thing to do was play peek-a-boo. He held up a blanket in front of his brother's face and said, "Where's Jordan?" Then his brother pulled the blanket down and giggled when Jordan said, "You found me!"

Jordan liked sharing some of his toys with his brother, too. He built a tall block tower for his brother to knock over and tickled him with a puppet. Jordan loved playing with his brother every day after school.

What Can We Do Together?

Draw black-and-white pictures. Newborns can't see very well, but one thing they can see is black-and-white pictures. Hold your pictures up in front of your sibling. They will probably want to stare at each picture for a minute or two!

Have a dance party. Put on your favorite music and dance around the room where your sibling can see you. With a grown-up's help, you can gently move the baby's arms and legs, or your parent can pick the baby up and dance around the room with them.

Read a book. Babies love hearing people's voices, so read your sibling a story! Your sibling won't understand how to pay attention to a book at first, but soon they'll learn to like them and will be excited to turn the pages.

Teach them new words. Point out everything you see and say the words out loud. You might say, "I see a tree. I see clouds. I see a car." Your sibling won't speak until they are about one year old, but they start learning what words mean from the very beginning.

Be a bath-time buddy. Play a gentle game of "splish-splash" with your sibling when they are in the tub, or gently pour water on their arms and legs. Be careful not to get water on their face!

What Do I Think?

Now that your sibling is here, you might be wondering about a lot of different things. Here are some questions you might want to ask your family, or you can write your own.

What will change about our family's routine?

Is there a special job I can have to help with the baby?

When will things go back to normal?

When will the baby learn to (walk, talk, read...)?

CHAPTER 4

GROWING UP TOGETHER

Before you know it, your baby sibling won't be a baby anymore! Once your sibling is walking and talking, they will be able to join you on all sorts of adventures. They will become an awesome friend. There are so many things to look forward to as your sibling gets older.

Being a Role Model

Did you know that your little sibling wants to be just like you? They probably think that you are the coolest person around. You might not realize it, but your sibling is learning things from you every day. You can be a super big brother and a role model for your sibling by setting a good example and teaching them to share toys, brush their teeth, and try new foods.

You can give expert advice for every new thing that happens to your sibling. You can help them through scary things like going to kindergarten, visiting the doctor, or disagreeing with a friend. It's been a long time since your parent has done kid things like losing a tooth, so you will be able to give special advice.

We have good news: Being a role model isn't all hard work! You can also be an awesome brother *and* have fun by just doing things you love with your sibling. If you love art, you can color with them. If you love sports, you can play outside with them (and maybe even let them win sometimes!). Whatever your favorite thing is, your sibling will want to do it with you.

Family Time

We've been talking a lot about the baby in this book, but this book is also about someone just as important . . . you!

One thing is for sure: A new baby will take up a lot of your parent's time. Your parent might be really, really tired. They might not have as much patience. These changes might make you feel sad because you miss your mom or dad a little. You might feel jealous of your sibling and wish you got as much attention as they do. You might feel bored because you have to play by yourself sometimes. You might wonder if your parent loves you as much as they did before. (Pinky promise: They do! They love you *so* much!) You might even wish things could go back to how they were before. All big brothers have a lot of very strong feelings when they get a new sibling, and that's totally normal.

Becoming a big brother means a lot of changes, but everything will get easier after some time. It's important to talk with your parent about how it feels for you to be a big brother. They can't help you if they don't know what's bothering you.

You can also look forward to special time alone with your parent. You could play a board game while your sibling naps. Or you could go on a fun date, like a trip to the museum. There are some things that only big kids can do. You'll get to do them alone with your parent! Together with your parent, plan some activities that can be your special time together.

What Can We Do Together?

As your sibling gets older, here are just some of the things you'll be able to do together:

Have a family movie night. Pick a movie together, pop some popcorn, and pile cozy blankets and pillows in front of the screen.

Make food together. Find a recipe in a cookbook and make it together. (Always ask a grown-up to help.)

Go to a playground. Ask a grown-up to take you to the playground for a game of tag or hide-and-go-seek.

Have a pretend tea party. Wear dress-up clothes, gather all your stuffed animals, and make food out of clay. Don't forget to pour some pretend tea!

Go for a swim. Head to family swim time at a nearby pool. (Always ask a grown-up to take you.)

Have an indoor campout. Gather blankets and sheets and build a tent in your living room. Pretend you're camping, make shadow puppets with a flashlight, and go to bed in sleeping bags.

Make a craft. Gather craft supplies like glue, paper, pipe cleaners, Popsicle sticks, or whatever you have in your house. Make something to give to your grandparent, aunt, teacher, or each other!

What Do I Think?

There's a lot to think about as you get used to being a big brother. These are some questions we had when we became big brothers, but you can add your own, too. Think about your answers or write them down. If you want, talk about them with your family afterward.

How do I feel about being a big brother?

What ideas do I have for special things I want to do alone with my parent?

What am I most looking forward to doing with my sibling when they're older?

What advice do I want to make sure I tell my sibling?

BIG BROTHERS UNITE!

Congrats! You are now officially a big brother. The Big Brothers in this book are *so* glad that you are now a member of our special club. We hope that our stories have shown you different ways to be a super brother.

You helped your family get ready for your new sibling. You learned how to take care of them and became such a good helper. You've thought about all of the fun things you'll be able to do together when you are both older. All you have to do now is enjoy time with your new sibling and keep growing up *together*.

Remember that if you ever need more advice, you can ask other big brothers (and sisters) in your own life. They might be friends at school, teachers, or even people in your own family, but there are big brothers all around you. Don't forget to ask them for help! And of course, your parent will always be there to answer questions, too.

Love,
The Brothers

Acknowledgments

A sincere thank-you to the grown-up who bought this book for a kiddo in your life. It is an honor and a privilege to be a small part of this special time for your family.

Thanks to Susan Haynes, Erum Khan, and the entire team at Callisto Media for inviting me to be a part of this project.

Thanks to Amy Chase, Alice Truscott, and Callum Borchers for providing me with big-sibling wisdom. Thanks to Addie, Ben, Charlotte, Emma, and Hazel: I imagine I'm talking to you every time I write something for kids! Thanks for being my inspiration.

Thanks as always to my parents and Dan for supporting everything I do, and to Juniper for giving me some firsthand "how to care for a new baby" material. I love you.

About the Author

Ashley Moulton has spent the last decade working in children's media at companies like Nickelodeon and YouTube and at her kids' cooking company, Nomster Chef. She is the author of *Let's Party! Kids Cookbook*, a cookbook with fun party recipes for kids, which was published in 2019.

Ashley graduated from Stanford's Graduate School of Education with an M.A. in learning, design, and technology in 2015, and from Ithaca College as a Park Scholar with a B.S. in television-radio in 2009. She lives in Philadelphia with her husband and daughter and loves cooking, travel, yoga, home design, and painting. Find her at AshleyMoulton.com.

CPSIA information can be obtained
at www.ICGtesting.com
Printed in the USA
JSHW040006110323
38770JS00003B/5